THE UNIVERSAL GUIDE TO GESTALT DESIGN PRINCIPLES IN ART AND PHOTOGRAPHY

CREATING MEANINGFUL VISUAL EXPERIENCES FOR 6TH GRADERS AND UP

FERDY SAITTA

QUESTQUILL BOOKS

CONTENTS

Preface   1

Introduction   4
    The significance of Gestalt Principles in visual perception and design
    A brief overview of the key Gestalt Principles to be covered in the book

Chapter 1: The Foundations of Gestalt Principles   7
    Explanation of Gestalt Psychology and its Pioneers
    Overview of the core principles: proximity, similarity, closure, continuation, figure-ground, and more

Chapter 2: Proximity and Grouping   10
    Detailed exploration of the Proximity Principle
    How proximity influences the perception of relationships and groupings
    Real-world examples in art, design, and everyday scenarios

Chapter 3: Similarity and Pattern Recognition   14
    In-depth analysis of the Similarity Principle
    How similarity creates patterns and visual coherence
    Case studies illustrating the use of similarity in various design contexts

Chapter 4: Closure and Visual Completion   18
    Comprehensive Examination of the Closure Principle
    How closure triggers the mind to complete visual information
    Showcasing artwork and designs that play with incomplete forms

Chapter 5: Continuation and Flow   23

A thorough exploration of the Continuation Principle

How continuation guides the viewer's eye and creates visual flow

Examples of how artists and designers leverage continuation for storytelling

Chapter 6: Figure and Ground   27

Detailed study of the Figure-Ground Principle

How figure-ground relationships impact perception and focus

Analyzing designs where foreground and background interact dynamically

Chapter 7: Common Fate and Movement   31

In-depth discussion of the Common Fate Principle

How common fate imparts a sense of movement and direction

Examples from animation, interactive design, and kinetic art

Chapter 8: Practical Applications and Case Studies   35

Applying Gestalt Principles to various design disciplines: graphic design, web design, industrial design, etc.

Case studies featuring famous artworks and designs that exemplify Gestalt Principles

Chapter 9: Cross-Cultural Perspectives on Gestalt   39

Exploring how cultural context influences the interpretation of Gestalt Principles

Examples of how these principles vary across different cultures and artistic traditions

Chapter 10: Evolving Gestalt in Contemporary Design   42

Adapting Gestalt Principles to modern design trends

Examples of how these principles are used in digital interfaces, branding, and multimedia

Chapter 11: Mastering Gestalt: Practical Exercises   46

A collection of hands-on exercises to apply each principle

30 Step-by-step tutorials for creating designs that incorporate Gestalt techniques

Chapter 12: Looking Forward: The Future of Gestalt Principles   61

Speculation on the role of Gestalt Principles in future design and technology

The potential of combining psychology, AI, and design using Gestalt concepts

Conclusion 64

Recap of key takeaways from each chapter

Encouragement for readers to apply Gestalt Principles in their work

Final thoughts on the enduring relevance of these principles in visual art and design

Thank You! 70

Appendices 71

Glossary of key terms

Recommended reading and resources for further exploration

PREFACE

The Gestalt principles are like rules that help us understand how our brains organize things we see. Imagine you're putting together a puzzle. The pieces might not make sense alone, but you see a clear picture when you combine them.

The Gestalt principles help explain why we see patterns and shapes when we look at things. They help us understand how our brain groups things that are similar, close together, or look like they belong together. So, it's like our brain helps us make sense of the world by following these rules, just like when we put together a puzzle to see the whole picture!

If someone has difficulty making these connections and seeing the patterns or whole pictures, it might be a condition called "Visual Processing Disorder" or "Visual Perceptual Disorder." This means the brain has trouble understanding or understanding what the eyes see. It can make it harder for a person to recognize shapes, colors, and other visual information. If a kid is experiencing these challenges, they need to talk to a doctor or a specialist who can help figure out the best way to support them.

Exercising with and applying the Gestalt principles can benefit kids with Visual Processing Disorder or Perceptual Disorder. These principles provide structure and organization to visual information, which can help these children make sense of the world around them. Here's how:

1. Simplifying Complexity: The Gestalt principles encourage simplification and clarity in design. By using basic shapes, clear lines, and distinct color contrasts,

kids with visual processing difficulties can more easily recognize and differentiate between elements in a design or image.

2. Enhancing Focus: The principles guide the viewer's attention to key elements in a design. For children with visual perceptual challenges, this can help them focus on important information without being overwhelmed by visual clutter.

3. Strengthening Pattern Recognition: Many kids with visual processing difficulties struggle with recognizing patterns and shapes. Practicing exercises related to similarity, proximity, and closure can help train their brains to identify similarities and groupings better, making it easier to recognize shapes and patterns in everyday situations.

4. Developing Visual Tracking Skills: Gestalt exercises like continuity and figure-ground perception can improve a child's ability to track visual information smoothly and follow lines or paths without confusion.

5. Building Confidence: As kids complete exercises that use Gestalt principles, they can gain a sense of accomplishment and improved self-confidence in their visual perception abilities.

6. Improving Visual Discrimination: Exercises that involve sorting objects based on similarities (similar to the similarity principle) can help kids practice discriminating between different visual characteristics, an essential visual processing skill.

7. Enhancing Visual Memory: Working with closure exercises can improve a child's visual memory by training them to mentally fill in missing parts of an image or shape, which can translate to better memory for visual details in everyday life.

8. Creating Predictable Patterns: Children who interact with designs following Gestalt principles experience a sense of predictability. This predictability can be comforting for those with visual processing challenges, as it reduces the uncertainty they might feel when interpreting complex visual scenes.

Tailoring the exercises to the child's specific needs and abilities is important. Consulting with a healthcare professional or educational specialist familiar with visual processing disorders can provide personalized guidance and recommendations for exercises that best support the child's development.

INTRODUCTION

The significance of Gestalt Principles in visual perception and design

HEY THERE! HAVE YOU ever looked at a picture or a design and thought, "Wow, that looks really cool!"? Well, the way things look and feel to us is all thanks to something called Gestalt Principles. These are like magic tricks that our eyes and brain play together to make things look organized and easily understood.

Imagine you're putting together a puzzle. You can see a clear picture when all the pieces fit just right. That's kind of like what Gestalt Principles do – they help our brains make sense of what we see.

Think about how you recognize your friend's face. You don't look at each part separately – the eyes, nose, and mouth. Instead, your brain puts them together to see the whole face. That's because of a Gestalt Principle called "closure." It's like your brain fills in the missing parts automatically.

There's another cool thing called "similarity." This is why you group things that look the same. Imagine a bunch of colored circles. If some are red and some are blue, your brain groups them by color. It's like having a red and blue team in your brain!

When things are close to each other, your brain thinks they belong together. It's like having friends who stand near each other in a class photo. The "proximity" principle helps your brain know what goes together.

Do you know how some things seem more important than others? That's the "figure-ground" principle at work. Your brain decides what's the main thing (the figure) and what's the background. It's like when you see a shape in clouds – your brain picks out the shape (the figure) from the sky (the background).

Have you ever noticed that some pictures feel smooth and flowy while others feel choppy? That's because of the "continuation" principle. It's like following a path with your eyes. Your brain likes things to flow nicely, making things look connected.

All these ideas help artists, designers, and even everyday people make things that look great. They use these magic tricks to make posters, websites, and even how a room is decorated! By understanding how our eyes and brain work together, we can make things that are easy to understand and look super cool.

So, next time you see something awesome and wonder why it looks so cool, remember the magical Gestalt Principles that make our world of visuals make sense!

· · · ● · ● · ● · · ·

A brief overview of the key Gestalt Principles to be covered in the book

THESE ARE THE SECRET rules that our brains use to make things look cool and organized. Imagine you're creating a puzzle with your brain – these principles help your brain put the pieces in just the right places.

1. Proximity: Things Stick Together. Imagine you have a bunch of colorful blocks. When you put the same-colored blocks close to each other, your brain thinks they're buddies. Proximity is like the "BFF rule" for shapes – if things are near each other, they're best friends in your brain's eyes.

2. Similarity: Friends Look Alike. Have you noticed that they seem to be in a team when things look the same? Imagine you have different stickers – some are stars, and some are hearts. When you combine all the stars, your brain sees a star team! Similarity is like the matching game your brain loves to play.

3. Closure: Filling in the Gaps. Have you ever looked at a puzzle missing a piece? Your brain is a pro at completing the picture! Closure is like a puzzle superhero – it fills in the missing parts to make things whole. Your brain loves solving mysteries, even in pictures!

4. Continuation: Follow the Path. Imagine you're on a fun path in a park. Your eyes love following the path. Continuation is like that path for your eyes to follow in pictures and designs. Your brain thinks smooth lines and paths are super cool, and it guides your eyes along them.

5. Figure-Ground: What Stands Out? Imagine you have a drawing with a person and a tree. Your brain decides who's the star (the figure) and what's the background (the ground). Figure-ground is like spotlighting the main character on a stage – your brain knows who to focus on!

6. Common Fate: Moving Together. Imagine a school of fish swimming in the same direction. Your brain sees them as part of a team with a common fate. When things move together, your brain thinks they're friends going on an adventure. It's like being in a parade!

These super cool Gestalt Principles are like brain rules that artists, designers, and even you use to make things look awesome. They're like magic spells your brain uses to organize and understand what you see. So, when drawing, designing, or just looking at something cool, remember these principles making your brain a creative genius!

The book explores these principles in detail, teaches how they work, and discovers how artists and designers use them to create amazing pictures and designs. Your brain is about to become a master of visual magic!

Chapter 1: The Foundations of Gestalt Principles

Explanation of Gestalt Psychology and its Pioneers

Ever wonder how our brains make sense of all the things we see? Well, a long time ago, some really smart people started studying how our minds put everything together like puzzle pieces. This cool study is called Gestalt Psychology!

What is Gestalt Psychology? Gestalt Psychology is like a super fun detective game for the brain. Instead of looking at just individual puzzle pieces, it studies how our brains see the whole picture. Imagine you're looking at a bunch of dots on paper. Instead of looking at each dot, Gestalt Psychology asks, "Hey, how do these dots become a picture?"

Meet the Pioneers: Max, Kurt, and Wolfgang. Let's meet the awesome detectives who started all this brain puzzle-solving. First, we have Max Wertheimer, who's like the leader of the detective team. Max noticed that our brains sometimes trick us into seeing things that aren't there. Like when you see a moving picture, even though it's just separate images.

Next, we have Kurt Koffka, the creative thinker on the team. Kurt believed that our brains put things together in a snap – like magic! He thought our minds don't just see things as bits and pieces; they see the whole story.

And don't forget Wolfgang Köhler! He's the one who studied chimps and discovered that they solve problems in their heads, just like we do. He thought that our brains are pretty powerful, and they figure out puzzles without us even realizing it.

The Whole is More than the Sum of its Parts. The pioneers of Gestalt Psychology realized something amazing: our brains are like superheroes that put things together in a special way. They said the whole picture is more important than just the individual parts. It's like when you make a sandwich – the yummy taste comes from all the ingredients, not just one!

Imagine you're watching a movie. It's not just about each scene but the whole story that makes you laugh, cry, or cheer. Gestalt Psychology says our brains are like that – they see the whole picture, not just the dots or pieces.

So, thanks to these super smart pioneers, we know that our brains are superstars at seeing patterns, telling stories, and making sense of everything around us. They're like puzzle-solving champions, and Gestalt Psychology is their secret codebook!

Remember, the next time you look at a picture, a poster, or even a cool design, think about how your brain uses its Gestalt magic to see the big picture and make everything fit together. Your brain is the ultimate puzzle master!

* * * * ● * ● * * *

Overview of the core principles: proximity, similarity, closure, continuation, figure-ground, and more

TODAY, WE'RE DIVING INTO something super cool: the core of the Gestalt Principles. These are like the secret codes that help our brains understand and organize what we see. Imagine them as your brain's helpers, ensuring everything looks right.

1. Proximity: Friends Stick Together. Think about your friends in school. When you sit together, your brain knows you're a group. That's how the "proximity" principle works. Things that are close together seem like they belong together. It's like your brain gives them a special high-five for being buddies.

2. Similarity: Birds of a Feather Flock Together. Imagine a bunch of toys – some are circles, some are squares. Your brain likes to put things that look the same in groups. It's like having a team of shapes! This is the "similarity" principle. When things look alike, your brain knows they're pals.

3. Closure: Filling in the Blanks. Have you ever seen a puzzle with a missing piece? Your brain fills in the blank to make the picture complete. That's "closure" – your brain loves finishing things. When something is almost complete, your brain magically adds the missing part.

4. Continuation: Follow the Path. Imagine you're hiking on a trail. Your eyes like to follow the path. The "continuation" principle is like a path for your eyes to follow. Your brain loves smooth lines that keep going. It's like a visual adventure!

5. Figure-Ground: What's the Star? Think of a magic show – the magician is the star, and the stage is the background. That's "figure-ground." Your brain identifies what's important (the figure) from the background. It's like finding a treasure in a sea of sand.

6. Common Fate: Imagine two teams playing soccer on a field. Your brain knows the players from the field they're on. This is "common fate." When things move in the same direction, your brain thinks they're part of the same gang. It's like following the same soccer strategy!

These cool Gestalt Principles help artists, designers, and even you when you're making something awesome. When you draw a picture, create a poster, or arrange your room, these principles sneak in and make things look organized and cool. It's like having a secret helper in your brain who knows how to make things look right.

So, the next time you see a cool design, try spotting these magic tricks your brain uses to make everything look neat and understandable. Your brain's like an artist that knows all the best tricks!

Chapter 2: Proximity and Grouping

Detailed exploration of the Proximity Principle

READY TO UNCOVER THE secrets of the Proximity Principle? It's like having a superpower for seeing how things belong together. Let's dive in!

What's the Proximity Principle? Think about your friends in school – when you're all sitting close, it feels like you're a team, right? Well, the Proximity Principle is a bit like that. The brain says, "Hey, these things are buddies because they're hanging out together!"

Friends Stick Together. Imagine you have a bunch of colorful shapes on a piece of paper. Now, if you put the same-colored shapes near each other, your brain thinks they're friends, like a group of red circles or a gang of blue squares. Proximity is like the "stick together" rule for your brain.

Making Sense of Designs. Let's say you're making a cool poster. If you put all the important info close to each other, your brain will know they're part of the same team. It's like giving them a secret handshake! Proximity helps your brain figure out what's connected and what's not.

Easy Navigation. Think about a website with buttons for different sections. When the buttons for "Home," "About," and "Contact" are near each other, your brain knows they're part of the same website gang. You can find things easily because of the Proximity Principle.

Avoiding Confusion. Proximity also helps your brain avoid confusion. Imagine a paragraph with sentences all squished together. It would be hard to read. But if you space out the sentences, your brain can read each part. That's the Proximity Principle making things readable.

Designers' Secret Weapon. Designers use the Proximity Principle to create organized and clear designs. When they want to show that some elements belong together, they put them close. And when they want to separate things, they give them space. It's like a secret language between designers and our brains!

So, there you have it, the Proximity Principle explained in a nutshell. Remember, whenever you see things close together in designs or pictures, your brain says, "Hey, these things are besties!" Keep exploring, and you'll uncover more awesome design secrets!

· · ● ● · ● ● · · ·

How proximity influences the perception of relationships and groupings

LET'S TALK ABOUT HOW "proximity" can make things look like best buddies or even part of a team. It's like magic for your eyes and brain!

The Buddy System: Friends Stick Together. Imagine you have a bunch of colorful shapes, like circles, squares, and triangles. Now, let's say you put the circles close to each other. What happens? Your brain thinks, "Aha! These circles are friends!" It's like having a secret handshake for shapes.

Finding the Gang. Think about your friends in school. Everyone knows you're a group when you all stand together, right? Proximity works the same way. When things are close to each other, your brain says, "Hey, these things belong together!" It's like having a team or a gang of shapes.

Reading Clues. Imagine you're looking at a page full of words. If some words are squished together, and others have space in between, your brain knows which words go together. It's like reading clues about how close or far apart things are.

Design Magic. Designers use proximity to make things look organized and neat. Imagine they're making a poster for a school event. They'll put the date, time, and place close to each other. That way, your brain knows all that information is important and connected.

The Space Trick. Here's a cool trick: designers can also use space to show things are different. Let's say they're designing a menu for a restaurant. They'll put the appetizers close together, the main courses close, and the desserts close. Your brain gets the hint that these foods are in their own delicious groups.

Avoiding Confusion. Have you ever seen a messy room? It's hard to find anything, right? Proximity helps avoid confusion in designs, too. When things that belong together are close, your brain doesn't get mixed up.

Making Sense of the World. Proximity isn't just for shapes and designs – it's everywhere! Think about your family. They're close to you, so your brain knows they're special. Proximity helps your brain make sense of the world around you.

Remember, when things are close in designs or pictures, your brain thinks they're pals. It's like a teamwork signal for your eyes and brain. Now you're a proximity pro – you know how to spot the buddies and the gangs of shapes! Keep exploring, and you'll uncover even more visual secrets!

• • • ● • ● • • •

Real-world examples in art, design, and everyday scenarios

LET'S JOURNEY INTO THE real world to see how the magical power of "proximity" shapes what we see and how we understand things. It's like having a special friend who helps us understand the world around us!

In Art and Design: Imagine you're looking at a colorful poster. The title, the date, and the picture are all close together. Your brain says, "Hey, these things are about the same event!" It's like your brain's super detective, spotting the connections.

Now, picture a comic book. The speech bubbles are close to the characters, showing who's saying what. Your brain doesn't have to guess – it's easy to tell who's talking. That's the power of proximity in action!

Designers use proximity to make things look organized and easy to understand. When making a website, they put the navigation buttons close together so you know they're part of the same team. Even a page layout uses proximity – like when a magazine arranges pictures and text close to each other to tell a story.

In Everyday Life: Think about your lunchbox – you put your sandwich, a fruit, and a snack close to each other. When you open it, everything's ready to be eaten. Your brain knows what's in your lunch gang, thanks to proximity!

And have you seen a road sign with an arrow pointing to the left and the words "Exit Ahead"? Those are close together to show you which way to go. It's like a map your brain understands instantly!

Even in a family photo, your family stands close together, showing you're all connected. Your brain says, "Hey, these people are special to you!" Proximity helps your brain see those special bonds.

The Proximity Party: Imagine you're having a sleepover with your favorite toys. You put your action figures in one corner, your stuffed animals in another, and your building blocks nearby. It's like having a party for your toys – each group of toys is like a gang invited to a different part of the room!

Proximity is like a secret helper ensuring everything in your world makes sense. From pictures and designs to everyday life, it's like your brain's saying, "Hey, these things belong together!" So next time you look at a poster or even arrange your toys, consider how proximity makes things organized and clear. You're a proximity pro now, ready to spot the buddies and the gangs everywhere you look!

CHAPTER 3: SIMILARITY AND PATTERN RECOGNITION

In-depth analysis of the Similarity Principle

GET READY TO EXPLORE the amazing world of the "Similarity Principle." It's like a cool brain trick that helps us group things that look alike. Let's dig in and uncover its secrets!

What's the Similarity Principle? Imagine you have a collection of stickers – some are stars, some are hearts, and some are squares. The Similarity Principle is like a rule that says, "Hey, if things look the same, they're probably buddies!" It's like having a secret handshake for shapes and colors.

Friends in Teams: Think about your crayons – when you put all the red and blue crayons together, your brain sees two teams of colors. That's the Similarity Principle at work! Your brain loves to make friends out of things that look alike.

Creating Patterns: Imagine you have a row of colorful beads. If you put the red and blue beads together, you'll end up with a cool pattern. The Similarity Principle is like a pattern-making magic trick – things that look alike make a picture even more interesting!

Designs and Logos: Designers use the Similarity Principle to make things look awesome. Imagine a logo for a sports team – if they use the same colors and shapes in different parts of the logo, your brain knows it's all part of the same team's spirit.

Even on a website, buttons with the same colors tell your brain they're connected. It's like giving each button a secret code that says, "We're all from the same place!"

Reading and Organizing: Have you ever read a book with different sections? When each section has the same heading style, it's easy to know where one part ends, and another begins. Your brain likes things that match, so it knows what's together.

Spotting Similarity Everywhere: Imagine you're at the park and see a group of birds – some are big, some are small, but they're all the same color. Your brain knows they're a bird gang! Even in your closet, when you put all your blue shirts together, your brain knows they're your blue shirt buddies.

So, remember the Similarity Principle next time you see things that look alike in a design, a picture, or even a group of friends. It's like your brain saying, "Hey, these things are all on the same team!" Keep exploring, and you'll discover more amazing brain tricks that make our world colorful and interesting!

· · · ● · ● ● · · ·

How similarity creates patterns and visual coherence

LET'S UNDERSTAND "SIMILARITY" AND how it makes things look cool and organized. It's like giving our eyes special glasses that let us see patterns and connections everywhere!

Creating Patterns: Imagine you have a box of colorful beads – red, blue, green, and more. Let's say you start putting all the red beads in one line, the blue in another, and the green in a third. Ta-da! You've just created a pattern without even trying!

Seeing the Magic: The magic ingredient here is similarity. When things look the same – like beads of the same color – our brain goes, "Hey, let's make a pattern out of this!" It's like a puzzle that your brain loves solving automatically.

Making Things Interesting: Imagine you're drawing a picture with different shapes – circles, squares, and triangles. If you put all the circles, squares, and triangles together, you're not just making groups. You're also making your picture look exciting!

Designing with Similarity: Designers use similarity to make things look super cool. Imagine a poster for a movie with stars in the background. If they use stars in the text and even on the border, they're weaving a starry theme throughout the poster. Your brain sees the pattern, and the whole design feels connected!

Finding Order: Remember a colorful puzzle you did? The pieces with similar colors were part of the same section. That's because similarity helps us find order in things. It's like assembling a puzzle where each piece belongs in a specific place.

Seeing the Big Picture: Imagine you're at the park, and you see flowers of different colors – red, yellow, and orange. Your brain sees the colors, and even though they're different, they create a beautiful pattern that makes the park look even prettier.

Cozy Clothes: Have you noticed that wearing a T-shirt the same color as your friend's makes you look like a team? Your brain loves seeing similarities, making things feel cozy and connected.

So, the next time you see a design, a picture, or even a group of things that look the same, remember the magic of similarity. It's like your brain making patterns and saying, "Hey, these things belong together and make our world even more awesome!" Keep exploring, and you'll uncover more secrets that make our eyes smile!

• • • ● • ● ● • • •

Case studies illustrating the use of similarity in various design contexts

GET READY TO PEEK into some exciting design stories where the magic of "similarity" makes things look amazing and organized. It's like looking at a bunch of cool puzzles that our brains love to solve!

Case Study 1: Awesome Movie Poster. Imagine walking by a movie theater and seeing a poster for an action-packed film. Look closely at the poster: the title, the characters' names, and the movie details all have the same style of letters. They're using similarity to create a pattern in the text! Your brain instantly knows that all those details belong to the same adventure.

Case Study 2: Fantastic Website. Picture this: you're exploring a website about animals. When you check out the buttons for "Cats," "Dogs," and "Birds," you notice something cool. All the buttons are the same shape, but each has a different animal picture. This is similarity at work! Your brain sees the pattern in the shapes and knows those buttons lead to different animal pages.

Case Study 3: Super Store Signs. Imagine you're at a mall and see signs for different stores. Check out the letters – they're all colorful and fun but have the same style. That's the magic of similarity! It's like having a secret code that tells your brain, "Hey, these stores are part of the same shopping place!"

Case Study 4: Book with Style. Consider a book you've read – notice how all the chapter titles are in the same font. Even though the words are different, the similarity in the font makes the book feel organized and put-together. Your brain can easily spot where each chapter starts.

Case Study 5: Team Spirit Jersey. Imagine you're on a soccer team, wearing jerseys of the same color and pattern. When you're out on the field, your brain knows that the players in matching jerseys are your teammates. The similarity in your jerseys creates a sense of team spirit!

Case Study 6: Happy Birthday Card Ever received a birthday card with different balloons on it? Even though the balloons are different colors, their shapes are the same. That's the power of similarity! Your brain sees the pattern in the shapes and knows they're all part of the birthday celebration.

So, remember these exciting case studies next time you see a movie poster, explore a website, or even pick up a book. When things look alike, your brain dances happily because it sees patterns and connections. It's like having a design secret that makes everything organized and super cool! Keep exploring, and you'll find similarity making the world more interesting and colorful!

Chapter 4: Closure and Visual Completion

Comprehensive Examination of the Closure Principle

It's time now to examine the "Closure Principle." It's like a brain puzzle that helps us complete missing pieces and see whole pictures even when they're not there. Let's jump in and uncover the secrets of closure!

What's the Closure Principle? Imagine you have a puzzle with one piece missing. Your brain doesn't just give up and say, "Oh well!" Nope, it loves solving puzzles, filling in the missing piece with magic. That's the Closure Principle – your brain loves to complete things, even if they're not in front of you.

Completing the Picture: Think about a connect-the-dots drawing. When you connect the dots, suddenly, you have a complete picture of a cat, a tree, or anything else. That's closure at work! Your brain sees the dots and can't resist joining them to make something whole.

Filling in the Blanks: Imagine you're looking at a drawing of a house, but the roof is left unfinished. Your brain doesn't like loose ends, so it draws an imaginary roof to complete the house. That's closure making the picture feel complete and neat.

Hidden Messages: Sometimes, artists use the Closure Principle to hide messages in their artwork. They might draw just part of a word or an image, letting your brain fill in the rest. It's like a visual treasure hunt!

Puzzles Everywhere: Have you ever seen a logo with a simple symbol, like the Nike swoosh? Your brain doesn't see it as just a shape; it sees the whole brand. That's closure – your brain knows the brand from a tiny piece of it.

Making Sense of Shapes: Imagine you're looking at a bunch of shapes – circles, triangles, and squares. If some shapes are missing parts, but you can still tell what they are, your brain uses closure. It's like your brain's special power to complete the shapes.

Your Imagination at Work: When you read a book, your brain creates images of the characters and places in your mind. It's like a movie playing in your head, thanks to closure. Your brain uses words to fill in the scenes and make the story come alive.

So, remember the Closure Principle next time you look at a puzzle, a drawing, or even read a book. Your brain is like a puzzle-solving hero, completing missing pieces and making things whole. It's like your imagination has a magical power to see beyond what's there and create amazing pictures in your mind.

• • • • ● • ● • • •

How closure triggers the mind to complete visual information

LET'S LOOK AT HOW "closure" works magic in our brains. It's like having a super-power that finishes pictures and puzzles for us. Get ready to uncover the secrets of how closure triggers our minds to complete what we see!

Finishing the Puzzle: Imagine you're looking at a puzzle with just a few pieces missing. Your brain is like a puzzle champion – it can't stand leaving things unfinished! So, it uses its special power of closure to fill in those gaps. Suddenly, you're looking at a complete picture, even if some parts are missing.

Connecting the Dots: Think about a dot-to-dot drawing. You start by connecting the dots, and boom! You have a picture. Your brain loves this game because it uses closure. It's connecting the dots in a way that makes sense, creating a whole new image.

Seeing Hidden Pictures: Sometimes, artists use closure to make us see hidden things. Imagine a drawing with just a few lines, and suddenly you see a cat or a flower. Your brain uses magical closure power to turn those lines into recognizable shapes.

Your Brain's Imagination: When you read a book, your brain goes on an adventure. It takes the words you read and turns them into pictures in your mind. You're like a director of your movie, using closure to imagine scenes, characters, and places.

Completing Familiar Shapes: Imagine looking at a drawing of a person's face. If the eyes and mouth are missing, your brain still knows it's a face. It uses closure to complete the missing parts with what it knows should be there. Your brain loves making sense of things!

Pictures in Pieces: Think about a logo you know, like the Apple logo. It's just a bitten apple, but your brain instantly knows it's Apple Inc. That's closure at work! Your brain completes the picture with the missing pieces it knows.

Visual Detective: Imagine you see footsteps on a sandy beach leading toward a treasure chest. Even though you don't see the person who left the footsteps, your brain uses closure to imagine the pirate or explorer who made them.

So, remember, closure is like a creative detective in your brain. It fills in the missing parts, finishes puzzles, and helps you see hidden pictures. It's like having a magical imagination that turns incomplete things into complete wonders. Keep exploring, and discover how your brain's closure power makes the world more exciting and imaginative!

· · · · ● · ● · ● · ·

Showcasing artwork and designs that play with incomplete forms

LET'S TALK NOW OF "incomplete forms" – a super cool trick that artists and designers use to make their work stand out. It's like looking at a half-finished puzzle and finding the beauty in the pieces that aren't all there and how incomplete forms make art and designs awesome!

Creating Mystery: Imagine you're looking at a drawing of a person, but their face is only outlined. Your brain goes, "Hey, what's missing?" That's the magic of incomplete forms. Artists purposely leave parts undone to create mystery and make you curious about what's not shown.

Feeling the Movement: Picture a painting of a bird mid-flight. The artist might show the wings and tail, leaving out the body. This gives you a sense of movement like the bird is soaring through the sky. Incomplete forms can capture action and make art feel alive.

Playing with Shapes: Think about a sculpture that looks like a person, but the head isn't fully formed. Your brain still recognizes it's a person, even with the missing part. Artists play with shapes to challenge your brain to complete the picture.

Leaving an Impression: Imagine a picture of a flower, but the petals are only suggested with a few lines. Your brain fills in the missing petals, creating a vivid image in your mind. Incomplete forms let you use your imagination to make the artwork even more special.

Design Delight: Designers use incomplete forms to make things look modern and stylish. Imagine a logo with a letter cut off – your brain knows what letter it is because of its shape. It's like a creative puzzle that your brain enjoys solving.

Hinting at Stories: Picture a poster with just a few brushstrokes of a city skyline. Your brain starts imagining the bustling city, the people, and the stories behind those few lines. Incomplete forms give you hints about exciting stories waiting to be discovered.

Your Turn to Explore: Now, it's your turn to be an art detective! When you see artwork or designs with parts that aren't fully shown, use your imagination to complete the missing pieces. You're like a co-creator with the artist, uniquely bringing the artwork to life.

So, the next time you spot a drawing, a painting, or a logo using incomplete forms, remember that it's all part of the creative magic. Incomplete forms invite you to join the artistic adventure and make the artwork uniquely yours.

CHAPTER 5: CONTINUATION AND FLOW

A thorough exploration of the Continuation Principle

THE WORLD OF THE "Continuation Principle." is like a magical path that our eyes love to follow in pictures and designs. Let's step onto this visual adventure and uncover the secrets of continuation!

What's the Continuation Principle? Imagine you're on a fun walk in the park with a smooth path ahead. Your feet naturally want to keep following that path. The Continuation Principle is like that –the brain's saying, "Hey, let's keep going in the same direction!"

Following the Path: Think about a drawing of a curvy line that starts at the bottom of the paper and goes to the top. Your eyes love following that line – it's like a journey for your eyes! That's the Continuation Principle making you want to keep looking.

Making Connections: Imagine you're looking at a row of dots, and a line connects some of them. Your brain wants to connect the dots that don't have a line, creating a picture or shape. The Continuation Principle loves connecting things and making them whole.

Flowing Lines: Picture a river winding through a forest. Your eyes enjoy following the river as it twists and turns. In the same way, the Continuation Principle guides your eyes along lines and paths in pictures and designs. It's like going on a visual adventure!

Design Magic: Designers use the Continuation Principle to make things look smooth and organized. Imagine a poster with lines that lead your eyes from one part to another. It's like a visual map that helps you explore the poster without getting lost.

Spot the Secret Paths: Sometimes, artists hide paths in their artwork to create surprises for your eyes. Imagine a painting with branches that lead you to discover a hidden bird. The Continuation Principle makes your eyes find these secret paths and explore the artwork more deeply.

Imagination in Motion: When you watch a cartoon, your brain sees pictures moving, even though they are separate frames. The Continuation Principle helps your brain create the feeling of motion as your eyes follow the frames one by one.

So, remember the Continuation Principle next time you're looking at a picture, a design, or even exploring nature. It's like your brain saying, "Keep following the path – something is interesting ahead!" Keep exploring, and you'll uncover more exciting ways your brain enjoys guiding your eyes along wonderful visual journeys!

· · · ● · ● ● · · ·

How continuation guides the viewer's eye and creates visual flow

CONTINUATION MAKES PICTURES AND designs feel like exciting adventures for our eyes. It's like following a magical path that leads us on a visual journey. Let's find out how continuation guides our eyes and creates amazing flows!

Follow the Visual Path: Imagine you're on a treasure hunt with shiny coins leading the way. Your eyes naturally follow the coins to find the hidden treasure. The Continuation Principle in art and design works similarly – it creates a path that your eyes love to follow.

Smooth and Satisfying: Think about reading a comic strip. The speech bubbles and pictures are arranged so your eyes move from one to the next. That's continuation! It's like a road that keeps your eyes moving smoothly and feels really satisfying.

Guiding Your Eyes: Imagine you're looking at a painting of a river. Your eyes start at one end and naturally follow the river as it winds through the painting. That's continuation guiding your eyes along the water's path, almost like taking a visual hike.

From Here to There: Designers use continuation to help you know where to look next. Imagine a website with a line that goes from a headline to a picture to a button. Your eyes easily follow that line, knowing where to go step by step.

Creating a Story: Picture a comic book page with panels showing different scenes. The way the panels are arranged guides your eyes from one action to the next, just like a story unfolding. Continuation helps connect the panels into a visual story.

Making Art Exciting: When an artist draws a picture with lines that seem to flow, like the curls of a wave, your eyes naturally follow those lines. It's like being on an artistic adventure, exploring the picture as your eyes go along.

Dancing with Colors: Continuation can also happen with colors. Imagine a row of flowers, each a different color. Your eyes may follow the colors like a dance, moving from one to another in a beautiful rhythm.

So, remember, continuation is like a tour guide for your eyes, showing them where to go and making sure you don't miss any cool stuff. It's like a visual journey where every step leads to something interesting. Keep exploring, and you'll discover more about how continuation makes art and designs feel like a fantastic adventure for your eyes!

· · · · ● · ● · · ·

Examples of how artists and designers leverage continuation for storytelling

READY TO SEE HOW continuation makes storytelling super cool? Let's go!

1. Comic Book Magic: Imagine you're reading a comic book. How the pictures are arranged guides your eyes from one box to the next. This is continuation at work! Your eyes follow the action, and you can easily understand what's happening in the story, just like watching a movie frame by frame.

2. Adventure in Panels: Each panel shows a different part of the story in a comic strip. The way they're placed helps you read the story step by step. Your eyes know where to go next, thanks to continuation. It's like having a map that takes you on an exciting visual journey.

3. Story Flow in Books: Picture a book with chapters. Each chapter might start with a special design, like a fancy letter or a picture related to the story. These designs use continuation to connect the chapters and make the book feel like a complete adventure.

4. Animated Movies: In animated movies, characters move across the screen, and your eyes follow them. The way characters move creates a continuation that guides your eyes, making the story come alive right before your eyes.

5. Website Adventures: Imagine exploring a website with sections like "Home," "About Us," and "Contact." If these sections have the same design or color scheme, your eyes easily know they're part of the same website journey. That's continuation helping you navigate the online adventure.

6. Picture Puzzles: Think about a puzzle that shows a person in different poses across its pieces. When you put the pieces together, the person is moving. Continuation in the puzzle pieces makes the picture tell a story as you complete it.

7. A Sequence of Images: Imagine a drawing that shows a girl running. The artist might draw her in different stages of her run – starting, running, and finishing. The way the images are lined up uses continuation to show a story of her movement.

So, whether in comics, books, movies, or even websites, continuation is like a guide that helps us follow the story path. It's like reading a map that takes us on an adventure step by step.

Chapter 6: Figure and Ground

Detailed study of the Figure-Ground Principle

The "Figure-Ground Principle." is like a super cool puzzle that helps our eyes figure out the main thing and the background in pictures and designs. Let's unravel the secrets of figure and ground!

What's the Figure-Ground Principle? Imagine looking at a picture where you see a shape and everything else around it. The Figure-Ground Principle is like your eyes' saying, "Hey, this shape is the important one, and everything else is the background."

Finding the Main Thing: Think about a picture of a tree with the sky behind it. Your eyes see the tree as the main thing and the sky as the background. This principle helps your brain figure out what's the star of the show and what's the supporting cast.

Making Things Pop: Imagine you're looking at a poster with bold letters on a colorful background. The letters are the figure – the important part you want to read. The background is like the stage, making the letters stand out and catch your attention.

Playing with Perception: Artists use the Figure-Ground Principle to play with how we see things. They can make us see one shape as the figure and then switch it, making the background the figure. It's like an artistic game that keeps our eyes guessing.

Seeing Shapes Everywhere: Have you ever seen clouds that look like animals? Your brain turns the clouds into the figure and the sky into the background. It's like your imagination uses the Figure-Ground Principle to create shapes from the world around you.

Designing with Balance: Designers use this principle to create balance in their work. Imagine a website with a picture of a phone on one side and text on the other. The phone is the figure, and the text is the background. This balance makes the website look neat and organized.

Seeing Both Sides: The Figure-Ground Principle can make us see different things in the same picture. Imagine looking at a vase, but suddenly you see two faces looking at each other. It's like your brain flips between figure and ground, creating multiple ways to see things.

So, remember the Figure-Ground Principle next time you look at a picture or a design. It's like your eyes' secret way of deciding what's important and what's the supporting cast. Keep exploring, and you'll uncover more amazing ways your brain uses this principle to make the world around you full of surprises!

· · · ● · ● ● · · ·

How figure-ground relationships impact perception and focus

Hey, curious minds! Let's examine the cool world of "figure-ground relationships" and how they make us notice things and focus on what's important in pictures and designs. It's like having a spotlight that shines on what matters most. Ready to explore? Let's go!

Spotting the Star: Imagine you're looking at a picture of a cat in a garden. The cat is the star – that's the "figure." The garden around it is like the background or the "ground." Figure-ground relationships help our eyes find the star of the show!

What Stands Out: Think about a white flower on a colorful background. Your eyes are drawn to the flower, and that's the figure. The background becomes less important, like a stage for the flower to shine on.

Catching Your Attention: Imagine you're in a crowded place, and you spot your friend wearing a bright red hat. Your brain sees the red hat as the figure, and all the other people become the background. The figure stands out, catching your attention.

Playing with Perception: Sometimes, artists use figure-ground relationships to make us see things differently. They might make a picture where you see two faces or a vase depending on how you look at it. It's like a visual trick that plays with your brain!

Seeing Hidden Pictures: Ever looked at clouds and seen shapes like animals? Your brain turns the clouds into figures, and the sky becomes the background. It's like a game of finding hidden treasures in the sky.

Making Design Work: Designers use figure-ground relationships to help you focus on important information. Imagine a poster with a big title and smaller details around it. The title is the figure, and the details are the background, so your eyes know where to look first.

Shaping Your World: Figure-ground relationships help you understand the world around you. When you see a playground with kids playing, your brain sees the kids as the figures and the playground as the background. It's like your eyes are detectives finding out what's going on.

So, figure-ground relationships are like special glasses for your eyes. They help you see what's important, just like focusing a camera on the main star of a picture. Keep exploring, and you'll notice how your eyes use this trick to spotlight the things that matter most!

· · · · ● · ● ● · · ·

Analyzing designs where foreground and background interact dynamically

LET'S JUMP INTO THE world of designs where the "foreground" (the main thing) and the "background" (the surroundings) play together like best friends. It's like watching a fun dance between the star and the stage. Let's check out how these two parts team up to make amazing designs!

Friendship of Figures and Grounds: Imagine you're watching a play. The actors on the stage are the figures, and the backdrop behind them is the ground. But what if the background changes as the actors move? That's what happens in designs where the foreground and background interact dynamically.

Moving Together: Consider a video game where your character runs through a forest. As you move forward, the trees and bushes move along with you. This dynamic interaction makes the game feel like you're exploring a magical world.

Layers of Fun: Some designs have different layers – like a picture on top of a colorful background. These layers can move, change, or reveal more as you look at them. It's like having a surprise hidden in different parts of the design.

Storytelling Magic: Imagine you're reading a book with pictures. The illustrations help you imagine the story better. Now, what if the pictures change as the story goes on? That dynamic interaction between the foreground and background shows you more of the adventure.

Animations That Wow: Ever seen cartoons where characters move against a changing background? The characters dance in front of a magical scene that transforms as they move. This makes the animation exciting and full of surprises.

Interactive Delight: In some designs, you can click or touch things to make them move or change. Imagine a digital book where you touch the characters, and they react! This dynamic interaction keeps you engaged and adds an extra layer of fun.

Magic in Advertisements: Have you noticed ads with things flying in and out? They might show a toy racing car zooming into the screen or a product appearing magically. This dynamic interaction grabs your attention and makes the ad memorable.

So, dynamic interaction between the foreground and background is like a secret dance that makes designs more exciting. The figure and ground are partners that create a lively performance for your eyes. Keep exploring; you'll find designs that surprise, move, and make you smile with their fantastic teamwork!

Chapter 7: Common Fate and Movement

In-depth discussion of the Common Fate Principle

GET READY TO EXPLORE the "Common Fate Principle," a super cool concept showing how moving things together can catch our attention. It's like a secret signal that makes our eyes go, "Hey, look over here!" Let's uncover the mysteries of common fate together!

What's the Common Fate Principle? Imagine you're watching a group of birds flying together in the sky. They're all moving in the same direction, almost like they're on a mission. The Common Fate Principle is all about things that move together, making our brains notice and pay attention to them.

Seeing Movement Teams: Think about a school of fish swimming in the ocean. They all move similarly, like they're part of a synchronized dance. This principle is like a spotlight on those fish, saying, "Hey, these guys are a team!"

Catching Your Eye: Imagine you're at a concert, and everyone claps simultaneously. Your eyes are drawn to the clapping because it's a common action. That's how the Common Fate Principle works – it makes us notice when things move in sync.

Animated Magic: In cartoons, characters moving together catch our attention. Imagine a group of characters running toward the same goal – your eyes naturally follow their movement. It's like the characters are sending a visual message with their actions.

Creating Patterns: Picture a marching band in a parade. They move together in perfect rhythm, a pattern of common fate. Our brains love patterns, so when things move in sync, it's like a puzzle we can't resist solving.

Safety in Numbers: In nature, animals move together to stay safe. Imagine a group of zebras running from a lion – they stick together for protection. The Common Fate Principle helps us understand that they're a united group.

In Design and Art: Designers and artists use this principle to create focus and impact. Imagine a poster where text zooms in together or circles move as one – it grabs your attention and makes the message clear.

So, remember the Common Fate Principle the next time you see a group of things moving together. It's like a visual alarm that says, "Hey, something important is happening here!" Keep exploring, and you'll notice how our brains love to follow movements on the same exciting journey!

$$\bullet \cdot \bullet \, \bullet \cdot \bullet \cdot \bullet \, \bullet \cdot \bullet \, \cdot$$

How common fate imparts a sense of movement and direction

THE WORLD OF THE "Common Fate Principle" gives us a special feeling of movement and direction. It's like being in a parade where everyone's walking the same way – it makes us feel part of something exciting! Let's explore how common fate gives us a sense of motion and direction.

Walking in Step: Imagine you're in a park and see a group of people walking together in a line. Your brain notices this because they're moving in the same direction, like a team on a journey. The Common Fate Principle works like that, making us feel like things are moving together toward a goal.

Dance of the Fireflies: Picture fireflies lighting up in a field at night. They're doing a synchronized dance when they all blink on and off together. This makes us feel like they're moving as one big group, even though they're small insects!

Zooming in Video Games: Have you played a video game where the characters rush toward a treasure? As they move together, your brain feels like they're all heading in the same direction. This sense of movement gives the game an exciting energy.

Animated Movies in Action: In animated movies, characters often move together in a certain direction. Imagine a group of animals running from one side of the screen to the other. This makes us feel like they're all going on an adventure together.

Creating a Rush: Imagine many people cheering at a sports event. When they all jump up simultaneously, it's like a rush of energy spreading through the crowd. This common movement makes us feel connected to the excitement.

Designing the Flow: Designers use the Common Fate Principle to guide our eyes. Imagine a poster where arrows point in the same direction. This creates a visual path that leads our eyes exactly where the designer wants us to look.

Feeling Connected: Our brains automatically feel connected when we see things moving together. It's like we're part of a team or a group adventure. This feeling of togetherness adds excitement to what we're seeing.

So, in real life, in games, animations, or designs, the Common Fate Principle gives us a special feeling of movement and direction. It's like a secret signal that our brains love to follow, making us feel part of something awesome in motion. Keep exploring, and you'll notice how this principle adds a thrilling sense of unity and action to the world around us!

• • • • ● • ● • • •

Examples from animation, interactive design, and kinetic art

LET'S EXAMINE HOW THE "Common Fate Principle" adds excitement to animation, interactive design, and kinetic art. It's like a high-five between things that move together! Ready to see some awesome examples? Let's dive in!

Animation Adventures: Imagine a cartoon where a group of animals runs through a forest. They're on a shared adventure if they all move in the same direction. This common movement makes the scene feel lively and full of action, just like a fun story coming to life!

Interactive Magic: Have you ever played a game where characters dance in sync with your moves? Imagine a game where you jump, and the characters jump with you. The Common Fate Principle makes them move together, making you feel like a team player!

Kinetic Art Creations: Think about a sculpture where pieces spin around each other with perfect timing. As they move together, they're having a playful dance. This dynamic interaction between the parts adds a sense of harmony and motion to the art.

Animated Emojis: Have you ever sent a message with emojis that move? Imagine a bunch of emojis clapping or laughing at the same time. The Common Fate Principle makes them seem like they all share the same joyful moment, adding extra fun to your messages!

Dynamic Websites: Sometimes, websites have buttons that change color or bounce when you hover over them. If all the buttons react similarly, they move together to welcome you. This creates a sense of unity and excitement when you explore the site.

Dance of Shapes: Imagine a screen with shapes that move in a pattern, like stars twinkling in the night sky. As they twinkle together, they're putting on a sparkling show. This common movement makes the scene magical and captivating.

Roller Coaster Thrills: In theme parks, roller coasters are like a real-life example of the Common Fate Principle. Imagine the cars moving along the tracks, going up and down. This synchronized movement creates a thrilling ride that makes everyone scream with joy!

So, the Common Fate Principle brings things together in motion, whether in cartoons, games, art, or even messages. It's like a team huddle in the world of visuals, making everything feel more exciting and united. Keep exploring, and you'll spot this awesome principle in various creative adventures!

CHAPTER 8: PRACTICAL APPLICATIONS AND CASE STUDIES

Applying Gestalt Principles to various design disciplines: graphic design, web design, industrial design, etc.

WELL, NOW! GET READY to discover how the awesome "Gestalt Principles" can be used in different types of design, making things look cool and work better. It's like having super design tools that create magic in everything from posters to gadgets. Let's see how these principles work in different design worlds!

1. Graphic Design Magic: Imagine creating a poster for a school event. Gestalt Principles help you arrange colors, shapes, and text to look great together. The principles guide you in ensuring everything fits well and catches everyone's attention. It's like piecing together a visual puzzle that everyone loves!

2. Web Design Wonders: Consider a website where you find information, play games, and shop online. Designers use Gestalt Principles to organize buttons, images, and text in a way that's easy to use. This makes your online adventure smooth and fun without getting lost in the digital maze.

3. Industrial Design Innovation: Ever seen cool gadgets, toys, or furniture? Industrial designers use Gestalt Principles to make them both useful and stylish. They ensure that the buttons on the remote control are easy to find or that a chair is comfy and looks awesome. It's like making everyday things super cool!

4. Packaging Perfection: Imagine going to a store and seeing colorful cereal boxes on the shelves. Designers use Gestalt Principles to create packaging that catches your eye and tells you what's inside. They ensure the design shows the deliciousness and fun waiting for you inside the box!

5. Clothing Creativity: Have you noticed how your favorite T-shirt has a design that feels just right? Clothing designers use Gestalt Principles to make patterns and colors work together. They ensure that the design feels balanced and fits well on your clothes.

6. Book Cover Charm: Look at the book covers next time you're at a bookstore. Designers use Gestalt Principles to make covers that tell a story before you read a word. They play with colors, shapes, and images to create a cover you can't wait to open!

7. Game Design Excitement: Have you ever played a video game and felt like you're in a cool world? Game designers use Gestalt Principles to create levels, characters, and interfaces that make the game engaging. They ensure everything looks awesome and guide you through the game's challenges.

So, whether it's designing websites, gadgets, or even clothes, Gestalt Principles are like a secret recipe designers use to make things look amazing and work smoothly. Keep exploring, and you'll notice these design magic tricks turning ordinary things into extraordinary experiences all around you!

• • • • ● • ● ● • • •

Case studies featuring famous artworks and designs that exemplify Gestalt Principles

UNCOVER SOME COOL CASE studies featuring famous artworks and designs that use the "Gestalt Principles" to create visual magic. It's like solving artistic puzzles that make things look amazing and interesting. Let's dive into these creative adventures!

1. Mona Lisa's Mystery: You've probably heard of the Mona Lisa painting, right? Look closely, and you'll see that her eyes seem to follow you no matter where you stand. This uses the "Figure-Ground Principle" – Mona Lisa is the figure, and the background seems to change as you move, creating a captivating effect.

2. Magic in M.C. Escher's Art: M.C. Escher was an artist who loved playing with your brain! Like "Relativity," his artwork uses the "Closure Principle." He tricks your brain into seeing impossible stairs going up and down simultaneously. It's like an artistic puzzle that keeps you guessing.

3. Google's Playful Logo: The Google logo seems simple, right? But it uses the "Similarity Principle" to make the letters look like they're having fun together. Each letter is a different color, but they're still on the same team. This design makes Google's logo stand out and feel friendly.

4. The Olympic Rings: The Olympic rings represent unity among countries. These rings use the "Proximity Principle" – they're close to each other, showing they're connected. The rings also use the "Common Fate Principle" because they're all linked, symbolizing teamwork in sports and friendship.

5. The Nike Swoosh: You've probably seen the Nike logo, right? It's a simple checkmark shape called the "swoosh." This design uses the "Continuation Principle" because your eyes naturally follow the curve of the swoosh. It's like a visual path that makes the logo look energetic and active.

6. LEGO's Building Blocks: LEGO uses the "Closure Principle" to make its logo interesting. The letters "L," "E," "G," and "O" are built with colorful blocks, but they're not complete. Your brain fills in the gaps, creating a playful logo like a puzzle waiting to be solved.

7. Picasso's Play with Shapes: Pablo Picasso was an artist who loved to mix things up. In his painting "Three Musicians," he uses the "Figure-Ground Principle" in a clever way. The musicians are made of colorful shapes, but their instruments blend into their shapes. Your brain has to figure out the puzzle of who's who!

So, these case studies show how famous artists and designers use Gestalt Principles to make their creations awesome and exciting. They're using creative tricks to catch your eye and make you think. Keep exploring, and you'll discover more art and designs that use these cool principles to add a touch of magic to everything you see!

CHAPTER 9: CROSS-CULTURAL PERSPECTIVES ON GESTALT

Exploring how cultural context influences the interpretation of Gestalt Principles

LET'S NOW ANALYZE HOW the culture you're in can change the way you see things. It's like having a special pair of glasses that make art, and designs look different based on where you're from. Ready to learn how cultural context shapes your view? Let's go!

Different Ways of Seeing: Imagine looking at a picture that shows a group of people. In one culture, they might see a happy celebration. In another, they might see a serious meeting. How people from different cultures understand the same picture can be like reading different stories!

Colors and Meanings: Colors can have different meanings in different places. In one culture, red might mean luck and happiness. In another, it could mean danger. So, when colors are used in designs, they might send different messages depending on where you're from.

Symbols and Messages: Think about symbols like thumbs-up or peace signs. While a thumbs-up might mean "good job" in one culture, it could mean something different elsewhere. Gestalt Principles can make these symbols look cool, but the meaning might change depending on your culture.

Shapes and Traditions: Shapes can also be meaningful in different cultures. A circle might symbolize unity and wholeness in one place, but it could mean something else in another. Designers must consider how different cultures might see them when they use shapes.

Designs and Customs: Imagine seeing a design with patterns that look familiar to your culture. It might make you feel connected to it. But someone from a different culture might see the same design and not feel the same way. Cultural context can make designs feel like home or like something new.

Languages in Design: Words in designs can be tricky too. A slogan that sounds awesome in one language might not sound as cool in another. Designers must ensure that their words work well in different cultures so everyone can understand and enjoy them.

So, remember that your culture is like a treasure chest of stories, symbols, and meanings. Gestalt Principles make designs look interesting, but your culture helps you understand them uniquely. Keep exploring, and you'll discover how these principles and your culture work together to make the world of art and design even more colorful and exciting!

· · · ● · ● ● · · ·

Examples of how these principles vary across different cultures and artistic traditions

LET'S JOURNEY INTO THE "Gestalt Principles" world and how they can look different depending on where and what art you're looking at. It's like having a bunch of cool art flavors from around the world! Ready to discover how these principles change across cultures? Let's go!

Colors in Different Places: Imagine a painting with lots of colors. Certain colors might mean happiness in one culture, but in another, they could mean something else. For example, red might be seen as lucky in one place but exciting in another. So, the same colors can create different feelings in different cultures.

Shapes Tell Stories: Shapes in art can tell stories, but the stories might change depending on where you are. A circle might mean unity in one culture, while it could represent something else in another. So, the shapes in art can have various meanings in different parts of the world.

Symbols and Traditions: Think about symbols like animals or objects. In one culture, a bird might symbolize freedom, but in another, it could mean something else. Even everyday objects might have special meanings in different places; artists use these symbols to communicate ideas.

Balance and Harmony: How things are arranged in art can also change. In some cultures, balance means having things equal on both sides, while in others, it might mean having a sense of movement. So, what looks balanced in one place might look different in another.

Text and Languages: Art can have words, but words can look different in different languages. A catchy slogan might rhyme perfectly in one language but not in another. Artists and designers must ensure their words work well in different cultures so everyone can enjoy the message.

Cultural Stories in Art: Artistic traditions and stories can be unique to different cultures. In one place, a pattern might tell a story about history, while in another, it could be about nature. Artists use these stories to create art that's meaningful to the people of their culture.

Emotions in Art: Sometimes, art expresses emotions, but emotions can be different in different cultures. A happy face might be understood the same way worldwide, but more complex emotions might have different interpretations depending on where you are.

So, think of Gestalt Principles as special art tools artists and designers use to create amazing things. And just like flavors change in different foods, these principles can look and feel different depending on the culture and art style you're exploring. Keep discovering, and you'll find that the art world is like a big, colorful puzzle with pieces that unite uniquely and beautifully across different cultures!

Chapter 10: Evolving Gestalt in Contemporary Design

Adapting Gestalt Principles to modern design trends

The "Gestalt Principles" can give a trendy makeover to modern designs. It's like giving classic design tricks a cool new style that fits today's world. Ready to see how these principles rock in modern design? Let's go!

1. Minimalist Magic: Imagine a design with just a few simple shapes and colors. Modern designs often love to keep things clean and simple. The "Proximity Principle" works by placing related things close to each other. In modern designs, this can mean giving your eyes a comfy space to rest while conveying the message.

2. Digital Delights: Interactive designs are all the rage in the digital world. The "Common Fate Principle" gets an upgrade here! Imagine buttons that light up when you hover over them or icons that bounce when you tap. This modern touch adds a playful twist to designs, making them fun to explore.

3. Bold and Vibrant: Modern designs often use bright colors and bold fonts to grab your attention. The "Figure-Ground Principle" works here by making important things stand out from the background. Imagine a poster with big, colorful letters – the letters are the figure, and the background supports their awesomeness.

4. Sleek Simplicity: Smooth lines and simple shapes are trendy in modern designs. The "Continuation Principle" works by guiding your eyes along paths. Imagine a smooth curve logo leading you from one end to the other. This creates a sense of flow and modern elegance.

5. Mixing and Matching: Modern designs like to blend different styles. The "Similarity Principle" comes into play here. Imagine a website with different sections with a unique look yet still feel part of the same family. This mix-and-match style keeps things interesting and modern.

6. Storytelling Swirls: Modern designs often tell stories through visuals. The "Closure Principle" gets creative here. Imagine a magazine cover with images that almost fit together but leave a little mystery. This makes you curious and encourages you to dive into the story.

7. Virtual Reality Fun: Modern technology lets us enter virtual worlds. The "Figure-Ground Principle" gives you something exciting to focus on. Imagine a virtual landscape where your eyes naturally follow a path that leads to a hidden treasure. This makes the virtual adventure even more thrilling.

So, think of Gestalt Principles as your secret design superheroes. They can adapt to modern trends, giving designs a fresh and exciting look. Like adding a cool twist to your favorite game, modern design trends give these principles a makeover that fits today's style. Keep exploring, and you'll see these principles shining in modern design, making everything look awesome and up-to-date!

· · · · ● · ● · · ·

Examples of how these principles are used in digital interfaces, branding, and multimedia

IN THIS BOOK SECTION, we will jump into the "Gestalt Principles" world and how they work their magic in digital stuff like websites, logos, and videos. It's like having a cool design toolbox for the digital world! Ready to see how these principles make digital things awesome? Let's dive in!

1. Website Wonder: Imagine you're on a website that's easy to use and looks great. The "Proximity Principle" is at play here. It groups similar things, like putting navigation buttons close to each other. This organizes the website and helps you find what you need without getting lost in the digital maze.

2. Logo Charm: Think about your favorite brand's logo. The "Similarity Principle" is working its magic. The logo might use the same colors or shapes in different parts, creating a familiar and memorable look. This helps you recognize your favorite brands even from a distance.

3. Video Magic: Notice how things move and flow smoothly when watching a video. The "Continuation Principle" guides your eyes along paths. This might mean video animations that lead your eyes from one scene to another, making the story feel connected and exciting.

4. Digital Unity: Imagine a game app where everything looks like it belongs together. The "Common Fate Principle" can be seen here. Characters and objects that move together give the app a sense of unity and make it a fun world to explore.

5. Social Media Style: Check out your favorite social media platform. The "Figure-Ground Principle" helps important stuff stand out. Imagine a post with a colorful background and bold text – your eyes focus on the words, making the message clear even in the busy world of social media.

6. Interactive Adventures: Ever used an app where things change when you tap or swipe? The "Closure Principle" plays a part here. Interactive elements like buttons or animations make you feel like you're solving a digital puzzle, keeping you engaged and having fun.

7. Streaming Coolness: Think about streaming platforms where you watch movies and shows. The "Common Fate Principle" shines when everything moves together, like the icons when you scroll or the way menus slide in. This makes the experience smooth and enjoyable.

So, whether you're surfing the web, playing games, or watching videos, Gestalt Principles are like your trusty digital sidekicks. They make digital interfaces look awesome, branding unforgettable, and multimedia exciting. Keep exploring, and you'll see how these principles give your digital adventures a touch of design magic that makes everything look and feel super cool!

CHAPTER 11: MASTERING GESTALT: PRACTICAL EXERCISES

A collection of hands-on exercises to apply each principle

GET READY NOW FOR some super cool exercises that let you use the "Gestalt Principles" to make your art and designs. It's like having a creative playground where you can create magic with colors, shapes, and more. Ready to try these out? Let's get started!

1. Proximity Play: Grab some colorful buttons, beads, or small objects. Arrange them in a way that groups similar colors or shapes close to each other. This uses the "Proximity Principle" and shows how things look organized when they're buddies. You've just created a colorful art piece!

2. Similarity Sketch: Take a sheet of paper and draw different shapes like circles, squares, and triangles. Now, color them using the same color for each shape. This uses the "Similarity Principle" – you're showing how things that look alike can make a design stand out!

3. Closure Challenge: Draw a half-finished drawing, like a puzzle with missing pieces. Use your imagination to complete the drawing by adding lines, curves, or shapes that make it whole. This uses the "Closure Principle" to show how our brains fill in the gaps and create complete images.

4. Continuation Creation: Draw a winding path or road on a piece of paper. Then, draw different objects along the path, like trees or animals. This uses the "Continuation

Principle" – the path guides your eyes as you follow the objects along the journey you've drawn!

5. Figure-Ground Fun: Get white paper and some black markers. Draw a simple shape, like a heart, and color it black. Then, create a background around it using colorful shapes or patterns. This uses the "Figure-Ground Principle" to make your heart shape pop!

6. Common Fate Challenge: Imagine drawing a group of people holding hands. Each person is a different shape or color but moving in the same direction. This uses the "Common Fate Principle" – the people moving together show unity and teamwork!

7. Your Own Design Adventure: Think of a cool design project, like making a poster, a logo, or digital animation. Choose one or more Gestalt Principles to apply to your project. For example, if you're making a poster, you can use the "Proximity Principle" to arrange text and images close together to clarify the message.

So, there you have it – a bunch of hands-on exercises that let you play with the Gestalt Principles. These exercises show you how to make your art and design more exciting and meaningful. Keep experimenting, and you'll discover how these principles are your creative superpowers that can turn your ideas into amazing visual wonders!

· · ● ● · ● ● · · ·

30 Step-by-step tutorials for creating designs that incorporate Gestalt techniques

TUTORIAL 1: COLORFUL PATTERNS with Similarity. You'll Need: Colored markers and paper.

1. Take a piece of paper and pick three different colored markers.

2. Draw different shapes like circles, squares, and triangles using one color.

3. Now use another color and draw the same shapes, but a bit smaller.

4. Fill the shapes with colors that match each other.

5. Keep drawing more shapes with the third color, making them smaller again.

6. Step back and see how similar shapes create a cool pattern!

7. You've made a vibrant design using the Similarity Principle. Great job!

Tutorial 2: Puzzle Piece Poster with Closure. You'll Need: Construction paper, scissors, and markers.

1. Cut out four puzzle piece shapes from different colored construction paper.

2. Arrange them on a bigger piece of paper, leaving spaces between them.

3. Draw lines connecting the edges of the puzzle pieces, like completing a puzzle.

4. Add details and colors to the puzzle pieces using markers.

5. Color the background around the puzzle pieces in a different color.

6. Stand back and see how the puzzle pieces look complete, even with spaces!

7. You've created a fun design using the Closure Principle. Awesome work!

Tutorial 3: Guiding Path Drawing with Continuation. You'll Need: Pencil, paper, and markers.

1. Draw a squiggly line from the paper's top to the bottom.

2. Draw different shapes like circles, triangles, and squares along the line.

3. Connect the shapes with your squiggly line, like a path.

4. Use markers to color the shapes in different bright colors.

5. Draw arrows pointing along the path to show the way.

6. Add little details inside the shapes, like dots or lines.

7. Look at how your eyes follow the path – you've made a design with Continuation!

Tutorial 4: Spotlight Art with Figure-Ground. You'll Need: Dark and light paper, scissors, and glue.

1. Cut out a big shape from dark paper, like a star or a tree.

2. Glue the dark shape onto a bigger piece of light paper.

3. Cut out smaller shapes from the light paper around the big shape.

4. Arrange the smaller shapes so they frame the dark shape.

5. Glue the smaller shapes down, leaving the big shape in the center.

6. Step back and see how the dark shape stands out from the light background.

7. You've created spotlight art using the Figure-Ground Principle. Awesome job!

Tutorial 5: Moving Collage with Common Fate. You'll Need: Old magazines, scissors, glue, and paper.

1. Cut out pictures of things you like from magazines.

2. Arrange the pictures in a line on a piece of paper.

3. Glue them down in a row, like a story.

4. Cut out small arrows from paper and glue them near the pictures.

5. Make the arrows point in the same direction like they're moving together.

6. Draw some lines connecting the arrows and the pictures.

7. You've made a cool collage that looks like everything is moving in the same direction – that's Common Fate!

Tutorial 6: Name Art with Proximity. You'll Need: Pencil, paper, markers

1. Write your name in big, bold letters using a pencil.

2. Choose a different color for each letter.

3. Draw smaller shapes near each letter, like dots, hearts, or stars.

4. Make sure the shapes are close to the letters they belong to.

5. Use markers to fill in the shapes with their colors.

6. Step back and see how your name looks colorful and connected!

7. You've created awesome name art using the Proximity Principle. Great job!

Tutorial 7: Symmetrical Creatures with Similarity. You'll Need: Colored paper, scissors, glue, and markers.

1. Fold a piece of colored paper in half and draw half of a funny creature.

2. Cut out the creature while the paper is still folded, making it symmetrical.

3. Open the paper to reveal your symmetrical creature.

4. Cut out smaller shapes from different colored paper.

5. Glue the shapes on one side of the creature's body.

6. Repeat the same shapes on the other side to make them look the same.

7. Look at your symmetrical creature – it's like magic using the Similarity Principle!

Tutorial 8: Animal Hunt Poster with Closure. You'll Need: Colored markers and paper.

1. Draw different animal shapes scattered around the paper.

2. Leave out parts of each animal's body, like a missing puzzle.

3. Add details to the animals, like eyes, tails, and ears.

4. Draw lines connecting the missing parts to the animals.

5. Use markers to color the animals in bright colors.

6. Color the background around the animals in a different color.

7. Step back and see how the animals look complete, even with missing parts – that's Closure!

Tutorial 9: Dancing Lines with Continuation. You'll Need: Markers, paper

1. Draw a curvy line across the paper from one side to the other.

2. Draw more lines that start from one end and end on the curvy line.

3. Make sure the lines have different lengths and angles.

4. Use markers to color the spaces between the lines in different colors.

5. Add some dots or small shapes on the curvy line.

6. Look at how your eyes move along the curvy line, following the continuation.

7. You've created a dance of lines using the Continuation Principle – it's like magic!

Tutorial 10: Shining Stars with Figure-Ground. You'll Need: Black and white paper, scissors, and glue.

1. Cut out different sizes of stars from both black and white paper.

2. Glue the black stars onto a white piece of paper.

3. Glue the white stars onto a black piece of paper.

4. Arrange the stars so they create a pattern, like a sky full of stars.

5. Glue them down, making sure the colors stand out from the backgrounds.

6. Step back and see how the stars shine in the night sky.

7. You've created a starry design using the Figure-Ground Principle. Fantastic work!

Tutorial 11: Connecting Dots with Common Fate. You'll Need: Pencil, paper.

1. Draw a bunch of dots on a piece of paper scattered around.

2. Divide the paper into sections using your finger or pencil.

3. Draw lines connecting the dots in each section, but ensure they go in the same direction.

4. Add more dots in each section and connect them with lines too.

5. Keep going until you have lines connecting all the dots.

6. Look at how the dots seem like they're moving in teams.

7. You've made a dot masterpiece using the Common Fate Principle – awesome job!

Tutorial 12: Nature Collage with Similarity. You'll Need: Old magazines, scissors, glue, and paper.

1. Cut out pictures of things from nature, like leaves, flowers, and animals.

2. Arrange the pictures on a big piece of paper.

3. Group similar things together, like all the animals in one corner and leaves in another.

4. Glue the pictures down, keeping the similar things close to each other.

5. Draw lines around the groups of similar things.

6. Use markers to add colors and details to the pictures.

7. Step back and see how your collage looks organized and full of nature – that's Similarity!

Tutorial 13: Design a Logo with Proximity. You'll Need: Pencil, paper, and markers.

1. Think of a simple word or your initials for your logo.

2. Write the letters close to each other, like they're buddies.

3. Add some simple shapes around the letters, like dots or lines.

4. Color the shapes and letters using bright markers.

5. Think of a cool name for your imaginary company.

6. Write the name near your logo using the same colors.

7. Look at your logo – you've made a stylish design using the Proximity Principle!

Tutorial 14: Mosaic Magic with Closure. You'll Need: Colored paper, scissors, and glue.

1. Cut out squares of different colors from colored paper.

2. Arrange the squares on a big piece of paper, leaving spaces between them.

3. Glue down the squares, making sure they don't touch each other.

4. Draw lines connecting the edges of the squares, like they're all part of a big puzzle.

5. Add some details inside the squares, like smaller shapes or patterns.

6. Step back and see how the squares look complete, like a colorful mosaic!

7. You've created a fantastic mosaic design using the Closure Principle. Great work!

Tutorial 15: Flowing River Drawing with Continuation. You'll Need: Markers and paper.

1. Draw a curvy line that starts at the top of the paper and goes down.

2. Draw different shapes like circles, triangles, and squares along the line.

3. Draw lines that start at one end of a shape and continue to the next shape.

4. Use markers to color the shapes in bright colors.

5. Add some dots or details to the line and shapes.

6. Look at how your eyes follow the line, like a river flowing through your artwork.

7. You've created a flowing river of art using the Continuation Principle – amazing job!

Tutorial 16: Shadow Play with Figure-Ground. You'll Need: Colored paper, scissors, and glue.

1. Cut out different shapes from colored paper, like animals or objects.

2. Glue them onto a bigger piece of white paper.

3. Draw shadows behind each shape using a pencil or a darker color.

4. Cut out the shadows and glue them down with space from the shapes.

5. Draw some details on the shapes to make them stand out.

6. Look at how the shadows make the shapes pop from the background!

7. You've made a cool shadow design using the Figure-Ground Principle. Well done!

Tutorial 17: Moving Creatures with Common Fate. You'll Need: Colored markers and paper.

1. Draw different animals or creatures on a piece of paper.

2. Add details like eyes, mouths, and tails to each creature.

3. Draw some lines that start from one creature and end on the next.

4. Make the lines go in the same direction as the creatures moving together.

5. Color the creatures using bright markers.

6. Use different colors for the lines connecting the creatures.

7. Look at how your creatures move as a team – that's Common Fate!

Tutorial 18: Super Sign with Proximity. You'll Need: Pencil, paper, and markers.

1. Think of a fun message or word you want to make into a sign.

2. Write the letters of the word close to each other, like they're holding hands.

3. Add small shapes or symbols near each letter.

4. Use markers to color the letters and shapes in bright colors.

5. Draw a big shape around the letters and symbols.

6. Color the big shape using a different color.

7. Step back and see how your super sign looks bold and awesome using the Proximity Principle!

Tutorial 19: Flying Friends with Similarity. You'll Need: Colored paper, scissors, and glue.

1. Cut out different bird shapes from colored paper.

2. Arrange the birds on a piece of paper, leaving spaces between them.

3. Cut out smaller shapes like circles and triangles from the same paper.

4. Glue the shapes onto the birds' wings and bodies.

5. Repeat the same shapes on different birds, like they all wear similar decorations.

6. Use markers to add details to the birds' eyes, beaks, and feathers.

7. Look at how your flying friends look like they're all part of the same bird squad – that's Similarity!

Tutorial 20: Puzzling Scene with Closure. You'll Need: Colored markers and paper.

1. Draw different scene parts, like trees, houses, and animals.

2. Draw only parts of each thing, like a missing puzzle piece.

3. Add details and colors to the parts you've drawn.

4. Draw lines connecting the missing parts to the parts you drew.

5. Color the background using markers.

6. Use different colors for each part and their background.

7. Step back and see how your scene looks complete, even with missing pieces – that's Closure!

Tutorial 21: Windy Path Drawing with Continuation You'll Need: Markers, paper

1. Draw a squiggly line across the paper from one side to the other.

2. Draw different shapes like circles, hearts, and stars along the line.

3. Draw smaller versions of the same shapes on the other side of the line.

4. Color the shapes using bright markers.

5. Add some dots or lines on the squiggly line.

6. Look at how your eyes follow the line like a path in the wind.

7. You've created a windy path of shapes using the Continuation Principle – terrific job!

Tutorial 22: Space Adventure with Figure-Ground. You'll Need: Black and white paper, scissors, and glue.

1. Cut out different shapes from black paper.

2. Glue them onto a bigger piece of white paper.

3. Cut out smaller shapes from white paper.

4. Glue the white shapes onto the black shapes, leaving a bit of space.

5. Arrange the shapes to make a scene, like planets, rockets, and stars.

6. Glue them down, ensuring the white shapes stand out from the black.

7. Look at your space adventure – it's like a journey through the galaxy using the Figure-Ground Principle!

Tutorial 23: Team Parade with Common Fate. You'll Need: Colored markers and paper.

1. Draw different people or creatures on a piece of paper.

2. Add details like clothes, faces, and hats to each one.

3. Draw lines that start from one character and go to the next, like they're in a parade.

4. Make the lines go in the same direction like everyone's walking together.

5. Color the characters using bright markers.

6. Use different colors for the lines connecting the characters.

7. Look at how your characters seem to be part of a happy parade – that's Common Fate!

Tutorial 24: Team Logo with Proximity. You'll Need: Pencil, paper, markers

1. Think of a cool team name or a group of friends you want to make a logo for.

2. Write the name or initials close to each other, like they're buddies.

3. Add simple shapes or symbols near the letters.

4. Color the letters and shapes using bright markers.

5. Draw a big shape around the letters and symbols.

6. Color the big shape using a different color.

7. Step back and see how your team logo looks strong and united using the Proximity Principle!

Tutorial 25: Sunny Collage with Similarity. You'll Need: Colored paper, scissors, and glue.

1. Cut out pictures of suns, clouds, and other sunny things from magazines.

2. Arrange the pictures on a big piece of paper.

3. Group similar pictures, like all the suns in one corner.

4. Glue the pictures down, keeping the sunny things close to each other.

5. Draw lines around the groups of similar pictures.

6. Use markers to add details to the pictures, like rays of sunshine.

7. Step back and see how your collage shines like a sunny day – that's Similarity!

Tutorial 26: Mysterious Scene with Closure. You'll Need: Colored markers and paper.

1. Draw different scene parts, like trees, buildings, and animals.

2. Draw only parts of each thing, like they're hidden in the shadows.

3. Add some colors and details to the parts you've drawn.

4. Draw lines connecting the hidden parts to the parts you drew.

5. Color the background using markers, making it look mysterious.

6. Use different colors for each part and their background.

7. Step back and see how your scene looks like a secret adventure – that's Closure!

Tutorial 27: Zigzag Journey with Continuation. You'll Need: Markers, paper

1. Draw a zigzag line across the paper, going up and down like a roller coaster.

2. Draw different shapes like zigzags, spirals, and waves along the line.

3. Draw smaller versions of the shapes on the other side of the line.

4. Color the shapes using bright markers.

5. Add some dots or lines along the zigzag line.

6. Look at how your eyes follow the line, like a zigzag journey.

7. You've created a zigzag adventure using the Continuation Principle – great work!

Tutorial 28: Shadow Play with Figure-Ground. You'll Need: Flashlight, objects, wall.

1. Place objects on a wall or a sheet of paper.

2. Use a flashlight to shine light on the objects from one side.

3. Watch as the shadows of the objects appear on the wall.

4. Move the flashlight around to see how the shadows change shape.

5. Experiment with different objects and see how the shadows interact.

6. Have fun making different shadow patterns on the wall.

7. You've created a playful shadow design using the Figure-Ground Principle!

Tutorial 29: Moving Train with Common Fate. You'll Need: Markers, paper

1. Draw a train on a piece of paper with cars and wheels.

2. Add details like windows, smoke, and the train's face.

3. Draw lines starting from the train's front and ending at the back.

4. Make the lines go in the same direction as the train moves forward.

5. Color the train using bright markers.

6. Use different colors for the lines connecting the train cars.

7. Look at your train –it's chugging along using the Common Fate Principle!

Tutorial 30: Circle of Friends with Proximity. You'll Need: Colored markers and paper.

1. Draw different people or creatures in a circle on a piece of paper.

2. Add details like clothes, faces, and accessories to each one.

3. Draw lines that connect each character to the ones beside it.

4. Color the characters using bright markers.

5. Draw a big circle around the characters, like they're huddled together.

6. Use markers to color the big circle using a different color.

7. Look at your circle of friends – you've created a close-knit group using the Proximity Principle!

Chapter 12: Looking Forward: The Future of Gestalt Principles

Speculation on the role of Gestalt Principles in future design and technology

Let's examine how the awesome "Gestalt Principles" might shine in design and technology. It's like imagining a new world where robots, gadgets, and designs become even cooler and more exciting. Ready to explore? Let's go!

1. Virtual Reality Adventures: Imagine entering a virtual world where everything feels real. The "Common Fate Principle" could make virtual objects move together like in real life. It would make the experience more believable, like exploring a magical land where everything is in sync.

2. Smart Art Displays: Picture a digital art display that changes as you move around it. The "Figure-Ground Principle" might make certain parts appear as you look from different angles. The art knows you're watching and changes just for you.

3. Futuristic Logos and Brands: In the future, logos might use the "Continuation Principle" in new ways. Imagine logos that come to life when you scan them with your device. Lines and shapes could guide your eyes through the logo's story.

4. Interactive Learning Helpers: Imagine studying with a digital tutor that uses the "Proximity Principle." It could group related information close together, making your learning super organized and easy to understand. It's like having a smart study buddy!

5. Personalized Design Experiences: In the future, designs might adapt to your preferences. The "Similarity Principle" could make designs change colors or shapes based on what you like. It's like having a design that becomes your friend and knows exactly what you love.

6. Design That Speaks Your Language: Imagine designs that use the "Closure Principle" to create shapes that look like letters from your language. It's like art and design speaking to you in a familiar and exciting way.

7. Robot Teamwork: In the world of robots, they might use the "Common Fate Principle" to work together smoothly. Robots could move and interact in ways that show they're on the same team, making tasks like building things or exploring easier.

8. Mind-Blowing Multimedia: Future movies and games could use the "Continuation Principle" to create seamless stories. Scenes might transition in ways that keep you hooked, like watching a never-ending adventure that guides your eyes effortlessly.

So, in the future, Gestalt Principles could be like the secret ingredients that make technology and design even more amazing. It's like a design treasure map that guides creators to make things look and feel awesome. Keep dreaming and imagining, and who knows what incredible worlds of design and technology you might help create!

· · · · ● · ● · · ·

The potential of combining psychology, AI, and design using Gestalt concepts

PSYCHOLOGY, AI (THAT'S LIKE smart computers), design, and Gestalt Principles come together to make some mind-blowing creations. It's like mixing magic potions to create super cool stuff! Ready to explore how all these things team up? Let's go!

1. Smart Art Helpers: Imagine having a computer that knows what makes your art look awesome. With the "Similarity Principle," AI could learn from your past designs and suggest colors and shapes you love. It's like having a creative friend who knows your art style well!

2. Emotion-Sensing Robots: Picture robots that can understand your feelings based on your expressions. With the "Common Fate Principle," AI could make robots move and react in ways that match your emotions. It's like having robot friends who get you and can cheer you up!

3. Custom-Made Learning: Imagine an app that helps you learn better. AI could use the "Proximity Principle" to organize information easily for you to understand. It's like having a digital teacher who knows exactly how you like to learn.

4. Designs That Understand You: Think about websites that change based on your liking. AI could use the "Closure Principle" to adapt designs to your preferences. It's like having a website that transforms to match your style and interests.

5. Storytelling Superstars: In the future, movies or games could change based on how you react. AI could use the "Continuation Principle" to make the story flow in your desired direction. It's like being the director of your adventure!

6. Mind-Reading Gadgets: Imagine a device that knows what you want before you even say it. With the "Figure-Ground Principle," AI could understand your thoughts and provide you with what you need. It's like having a magical device that knows you inside and out.

7. Super Smart Logos: Picture logos that change based on people's liking. AI could use the "Figure-Ground Principle" to make logos that stand out to different people. It's like a logo that becomes a chameleon, adapting to capture everyone's attention.

So, the possibilities are endless when psychology, AI, and design mix with the amazing Gestalt Principles! It's like having a big creative playground where ideas come to life in ways we've never imagined. Keep dreaming, and who knows what fantastic creations you might help bring to the world one day!

CONCLUSION

Recap of key takeaways from each chapter

Chapter 1: The Foundations of Gestalt Principles:

- Gestalt Psychology helps us understand how our minds work when we look at designs.

- Important principles include proximity, similarity, closure, continuation, figure-ground, and more.

Chapter 2: Proximity and Grouping:

- Proximity Principle: Things close to each other seem related.

- It helps us see how things are grouped in designs.

- We see this in art, design, and everyday things like magazines.

Chapter 3: Similarity and Pattern Recognition:

- Similarity Principle: Similar things look like they're a team.

- It creates patterns and makes designs look nice and organized.

- We find this in logos, patterns, and lots of different designs.

Chapter 4: Closure and Visual Completion:

- Closure Principle: Our brains finish incomplete things.

- It's like solving a puzzle in our minds.

- Artists use this to make cool designs that look complete, even if they're not.

Chapter 5: Continuation and Flow:

- Continuation Principle: The way things are lined up guides our eyes.

- It makes designs feel smooth and easy to follow.

- Artists use this to create paths for our eyes in their artwork.

Chapter 6: Figure and Ground:

- Figure-Ground Principle: One thing stands out from the background.

- It makes things look important and easy to see.

- Artists use this to make things pop in their artwork.

Chapter 7: Common Fate and Movement:

- Common Fate Principle: Things that move together look like a team.

- It makes art, and designs feel like they're moving and working together.

- We see this in animations and interactive designs.

Chapter 8: Practical Applications and Case Studies:

- We can use Gestalt Principles in graphic design, web design, and more.

- Famous artworks show how these principles make designs great.

Chapter 9: Cross-Cultural Perspectives on Gestalt:

- Different cultures interpret Gestalt Principles in their special ways.

- Designs can look different in various parts of the world.

Chapter 10: Evolving Gestalt in Contemporary Design:

- We can use these principles in modern designs like digital interfaces and logos.

- They help us make designs that look awesome in today's world.

Chapter 11: Mastering Gestalt: Practical Exercises:

- We can practice using these principles with fun exercises and step-by-step tutorials.

- It's like learning to create our amazing designs.

Chapter 12: Looking Forward: The Future of Gestalt Principles:

- These principles will keep being awesome in the future, even with new technology.

- We can use psychology, AI, and design to make cool things.

· · · ● · ● · · ·

Encouragement for readers to apply Gestalt Principles in their work

YOU'VE JUST EMBARKED ON an incredible journey learning about Gestalt Principles and how they make art, design, and technology pop with awesomeness. Now, it's time to take all that cool knowledge and use it in your very own creative projects. Ready for some encouragement? Let's do this!

1. Be Curious and Brave: Remember, every artist and designer started by trying new things. Don't be afraid to experiment with the Gestalt Principles you've learned. It's like playing with your favorite toys – you'll discover amazing ways to make your creations look fantastic!

2. Mix and Match: These principles are your secret tools. You can use them together or try one at a time. Imagine you're a magician creating a spell using different ingredients. Mix up the principles to make your designs truly unique.

3. Practice Makes Perfect: Just like riding a bike or playing a video game, improving at using these principles takes practice. Start with small projects and see how applying the principles changes the way your art looks. You're getting closer to becoming a design wizard each time you practice!

4. Trust Your Creativity: You've got an amazing imagination, and that's your most powerful tool. Don't be afraid to think outside the box and develop your creative ideas. You're the boss of your designs, and the Gestalt Principles are your magical helpers.

5. Learn from Everything: Whenever you see art, designs, or even cool websites, try to spot how the Gestalt Principles are used. It's like being a detective looking for hidden clues. Learning from other people's work can inspire your masterpieces!

6. Share Your Creations: Whether it's a drawing, a poster, or a digital creation, don't keep your awesome work to yourself. Please share it with friends, family, and even online communities. You'll be surprised by the positive reactions you get and the new ideas you'll spark.

7. Have Fun and Keep Exploring: Remember, the most important thing is to enjoy yourself! The Gestalt Principles are here to make your creative journey exciting and fun. Keep exploring, trying new things, and growing as a fantastic artist or designer.

So, let these words be your encouragement to dive into your creative world with confidence. Use the Gestalt Principles as your magical guide, and watch how your art and designs become more captivating, exciting, and unique. You have the power to create something amazing, and the world can't wait to see it! Keep creating and keep shining, you artistic superstar!

· · · · ● · ● · ● · ·

Final thoughts on the enduring relevance of these principles in visual art and design

As we wrap up our adventure into Gestalt Principles, let's chat about why these magical rules are here to stay in the land of visual art and design. Think of it like a super cool video game's final level–we're reaching the big conclusion. Let's dive in!

1. Timeless Treasure: These Gestalt Principles are timeless, like your favorite stories. They've been around for a long time, helping artists and designers create amazing things. And guess what? They'll keep being awesome for many years to come.

2. Universal Language: Think of the Gestalt Principles as a secret language that all artists and designers understand. No matter where you go, these principles help people communicate through art and designs. It's like having a code that everyone can read.

3. Creativity Booster: No matter how technology changes or how fancy designs become, these principles will always spark your creativity. They're like a never-ending source of inspiration that helps you make your art and designs more exciting and special.

4. Design Toolbox: Imagine you're a superhero with a utility belt full of gadgets. Well, these principles are like the coolest gadgets in your creative toolbox. They help you solve design puzzles and make your creations look awesome, no matter what you're working on.

5. New Adventures: As you grow and learn, you'll find new ways to use these principles. Maybe you'll combine or use them uniquely to create things we can't even imagine today. The future is full of exciting adventures; these principles will be your trusty companions.

6. Endless Possibilities: Art and design are about expressing yourself and sharing ideas. The Gestalt Principles give you endless possibilities to do that. They're like a treasure chest of options, helping you make your mark on the world.

7. Your Design Legacy: Imagine your designs becoming part of the world's visual history. Like famous paintings and iconic logos, your creations could inspire others for generations. And guess what? These principles will still be right there, making your designs shine.

So, as you continue your journey through art and design, remember that these Gestalt Principles are like your loyal companions. They'll walk alongside you, helping you turn your ideas into beautiful creations that capture hearts and minds. Keep creating, keep exploring, and use these magical rules to make your mark on the colorful canvas of the world!

THANK YOU!

APPENDICES

Glossary of key terms

1. Gestalt Principles: These special rules help us understand how we see and understand things, like art and designs. They make things look awesome and interesting!

2. Psychology: This is like peeking into our brains to understand how our minds work and why we think and feel certain ways.

3. Principles: These are important rules that guide our actions. It's like a map to help us get to where we want.

4. Proximity: When things are close to each other, our brains think they belong together. It's like friends standing next to each other.

5. Similarity: Things that look alike seem part of a team. It's like when everyone wears the same color shirt for a group photo.

6. Closure: Our brains finish things even if they're not all there. It's like guessing the end of a story even if you haven't read it all.

7. Continuation: How things are lined up guides our eyes in a certain direction. It's like following arrows to go on a special path.

8. Figure-Ground: One thing stands out from the background. It's like the star of a show shining on a colorful stage.

9. Common Fate: When things move together, they look like they're working as a team. It's like everyone playing the same game at a party.

10. Virtual Reality: Imagine wearing special goggles to step into a pretend world that feels real. It's like being in a dream you can touch!

11. Interactive: When things react when you touch or do something. It's like a game where the characters talk to you.

12. Technology: Fancy machines, gadgets, and cool stuff people create to make life better and more exciting.

13. Creative: Being super imaginative and making unique and exciting things.

14. Design: Planning and making things look cool, like logos, posters, or video game characters.

15. Inspire: When something excites you and gives you cool ideas to try out yourself.

16. Treasure Chest: Like a magical box filled with valuable things, it's full of knowledge and ideas instead of gold!

17. Enduring: Something that lasts long and never goes out of style. Like a classic storybook, you love to read it again and again.

· · · ● · ● · ● · · ·

Recommended reading and resources for further exploration

1. **"THE ART BOOK for Children" by Amanda Renshaw** is like a magical tour of famous artworks from different times and places. It's easy to understand and full of cool facts about art!

2. **"The Ultimate Book of Kid Concoctions" by John E. Thomas and Danita Pagel:** If you love creating things, this book is perfect! It's like a recipe book for fun crafts and experiments you can do at home.

3. "Art for Kids: Drawing" by Kathryn Temple: If you want to improve at drawing, this book is like a friendly guide. It has step-by-step instructions to help you draw all sorts of things!

4. "The Dot" by Peter H. Reynolds is about a girl who learns that even a simple dot can be turned into amazing art. It's a fun way to see how creativity works.

5. Websites and Videos: Check out websites like Khan Academy Kids, which has interactive lessons on art and design. YouTube also has art channels like "Art for Kids Hub" that show you how to draw awesome stuff step by step!

6. Visit Museums and Art Galleries: If you're lucky enough to visit a museum or art gallery, explore! You'll see real artworks and discover more about different artists and their styles.

7. Experiment with Your Ideas: Imagination is your best tool! Try different art materials, draw, paint, and create things you love. Every time you experiment, you're learning something new!

8. Ask Your Art Teachers and Librarians: Ask your art teacher or local librarian for book recommendations or resources. They're there to help you find exciting ways to learn more about art and creativity.

9. Explore Online Art Communities: Websites like DeviantArt and Behance are online communities where artists share their work. You can see different styles and even share your creations!

10. Keep Dreaming and Creating: The most important thing is to keep curious and creating. Whether drawing, crafting, or exploring digital art, you're becoming a better artist every time you make something!

Remember, exploring art and creativity is like going on an exciting adventure. Keep reading, trying new things, and having fun with your artistic journey!